Hey Parents!

We're Duy and Hien, the husband and wife behind Nightingale Baby.

Sign language stops billions of tantrums in their tracks, quells millions of meltdowns, and soothes upset babies around the world... but it also helps us understand and connect with our pre-verbal children in a deeper and more meaningful way. So, we created this book with the hopes that it will make communicating with your little one(s) just a little bit easier and a lot more fun.

We hope you read this story of Gale and the Baby with your kids, learn to sign together, and have some fun!

At Nightingale, we are committed to helping parents take care of their babies during the first years of life. We make products ranging from ultra comfortable blankets, swaddles to buttery soft bibs. From time to time, we enjoy doing projects like this sign language book too! They let us see the super talented side of our awesome team members and remind us of why we're doing this in the first place.

We would LOVE for you to tag us on Instagram @_nightingalebaby so we can be a part of your story with sign language!

Gale and Oscar Learn to Sign

A SIGN-ALONG STORY FOR PARENTS AND CHILDREN

Nightingale

help

Gale is the best **help** with the baby every day.

Oscar is too small to talk, but still has things to say.

eat

Oscar and Gale know how to sign words using just their hands.

When Oscar's hungry, he signs **eat** and Gale understands!

more

A noodle will do perfectly, Gale shares one from her bowl.

But Oscar quickly asks for **more**, eating the first one whole.

milk

"Oscar's thirsty," Gale thinks, "I'll get our favorite cup."

and carefully pours a glass of **milk**, filling it right up.

all done

When Oscar's belly is all full, Oscar signs *"**all done**"*,

Gale knows that now it's time to have some bathtime fun.

play

With bubbles, giggles, toys and soap they scrub and splash and **play**.

Bath time is their favorite way to end a busy day.

bed

With bath time done Gale helps get Oscar off to **bed**.

Teeth get brushed, pajamas on, their favorite story read.

clean

Now to the bedroom both kids go, it's messy from the day,

Gales knows it's time to **clean** and put the toys away.

smile

She sings the special clean up song that she and Oscar know,

And Oscar watches happily, while his **smile** starts to grow.

toy

Gale grabs **toys**, while Oscar makes noise - the two are quite the pair.

But soon enough the room is clean, with a little time to spare.

thank you

Gale's done the best job and gets rewarded, too.

When baby gives a big wet kiss and signs the words **thank you**.

sleep

But now sleepy eyes and sleepy sighs give way to a great big yawn.

Both the kids soon fall **asleep** now that their day is done.

Milestones

Photos

Milestones

Notes

Dates to Remember - Baby's Firsts

help	all done	smile
eat	play	toy
more	bed	thank you
milk	clean	sleep

American Sign Language (ASL) in the Book

help

eat

more

milk

all done

play

bed

clean

smile

toy

thank you

sleep

Coloring Time!

About Us

Duy Nguyen & Hien Hoang

When we're not busy working on bibs & blankets, or being with our two kids, we usually to come up with different quirky ideas to make playtime with them more interesting and memorable. This book started as one of those ideas.

Eliya Finkelstein & Cajun Abdel Wahhab

Husband and wife dynamic duo and the parents of two awesome kids. We see every day as an opportunity to impress our kids with another impromptu rap battle (Cajun always wins) and delight in cold mac & cheese.

Tris Lintag

A bespectacled lady who loves to draw, paint, and draw some more. She's worked both freelance and in corporate as an illustrator and graphic designer before being spotted by us at Nightingale. Nowadays, she makes designs and cute illustrations for kids and their parents with the rest of our team!